IGUANAS

IGUANAS

DON PATTON

THE CHILD'S WORLD

The iguana sits on the rock, as still as a statue, the sun's rays warming its body as it stares off into the distance. Many millions of years separate it from its reptilian ancestors, yet it remains mostly unchanged. Scales guard its entire body, and the five toes on each foot are equipped with long, sharp claws. Just below and behind the lizard's eye is a circular patch—an external eardrum. A ridge or crest runs along the iguana's back and long tail. The tail is used for balance during fast runs or to help with swimming when the animal takes to the water.

Sometimes, though, things aren't quite as simple as they seem. Even though the iguana still looks like its ancient relatives, it has developed some complex behaviors that allow it to survive in a wide range of environments.

There are 700 different species of iguana in the world—forty within the United States. Except for three species, all of these iguanas are *New World* lizards, living in North, Central, or South America. Iguanas are also common on the Caribbean Islands and the Galapagos Islands.

Iguanas range in size from the small *short-horned lizard* (only four to six inches long) to the large *common iguana* (up to six feet long). Most iguanas are eight to fifteen inches in length. The iguana's tail is usually twice as long as the rest of its body.

The areas, or *habitats*, where iguanas live are usually dense jungles or tropical forests. There, they may live in the trees but are also comfortable moving and feeding along the forest floor. They seem to prefer areas near streams and are very good swimmers. When threatened, they often drop off tree branches and into the water to make their escape.

Most iguanas are extremely *territorial*, which means that each lizard guards and defends an area it has claimed. When another iguana enters its territory, the defender raises itself on its front legs and moves up and down—somewhat like a human doing push-ups. The defender also stiffens a flap of skin, called a *throat fan,* under its mouth. An iguana may even lash at an intruder with its sharp tail.

Most iguanas are vegetarians, preferring to eat fruits, berries, and tender leaves. *Common iguanas*, which live in the jungles of Central and South America, eat mostly insects when young, but switch to a vegetarian diet as they become adults. *Land iguanas*, which live in the hot, dry environment of the Galapagos Islands, eat cactus! They also rely on cactus as their main source of water.

The native people of Central and South America use iguanas as a source of food. The meat of an iguana is white and tender and is said to taste like chicken or frogs' legs. A large common iguana provides enough meat to feed a small family.

After mating, the female iguana begins to search for some soft ground so she can build a nest. When she is ready to lay her eggs, she digs a hole in the soil with her nose. After laying the eggs, she covers them loosely with soil and leaves them unprotected. As the sun warms the ground, the eggs are incubated and continue to develop. When the iguanas finally hatch, they must take care of themselves right from the start.

In colder climates, female iguanas may hold the eggs within their bodies until they are ready to hatch. Once they hatch, however, these babies are also left to fend for themselves.

The *horned lizards* of the southwestern United States are quite different from most other iguanas. They are sometimes called *horned toads*, because their short, fat bodies make them look more like toads than like lizards. They have ten to twelve sharp spines that cover their bodies, protecting them from snakes and mammals that try to eat them. Horned lizards are quite fast when frightened, but if one is cornered it can puff up its body with air to make itself look larger. This also causes other

spines on the animal to stand erect. If this doesn't scare off the predator, the horned lizard squirts blood at its enemy from a gland in its eye! These actions usually discourage even the most determined predator.

Horned lizards live mostly in dry desert areas and rely on insects and ants as their main sources of food. They get their water by licking dew from desert plants in the early morning hours.

The *marine iguana* of the Galapagos Islands is another interesting lizard that doesn't live a normal iguana life. A good swimmer and diver, the marine iguana can hold its breath for up to ten minutes as it searches for food. It eats algae and seaweed that grow on rocks in the shallow ocean waters near shore. The marine iguana keeps its body warm during these cold-water dives by slowing its heartbeat. The blood flow inside the iguana also slows down, so that the iguana's body takes longer to cool. Even so, the marine iguana can stand only short periods in the water, after which it must sun itself on a rock to warm its cool body.

The *marine iguana* gets its water by drinking sea-water. The lizard has special glands that remove the salt from the bloodstream, and it blows the excess salt out through its nose.

About 360 million years ago, the iguana's lizard-like ancestors roamed a land covered by plants and insects. Insects were a plentiful food source. Millions of years passed, and the competition increased for available food and habitats. This competition caused the large variety of lizards we see today, as different species adapted to new habitats, new food sources, and new climates. This wide range of adaptations is shown by the 700 species of iguanas that live in the New World. From the strange horned lizard to the common iguana to the resourceful marine iguana, all have been able to adjust to their very different environments. The iguana is a survivor!

INDEX

PHOTO RESEARCH
Jim Rothaus / James R. Rothaus & Associates

PHOTO EDITOR
Robert A. Honey / Seattle

PHOTO CREDITS
COMSTOCK: front cover,2,27
Kevin Schafer : 4
Norbert Wu: 7,8,11,14,17,18
RON KIMBALL STOCK AGENCY: 13
Joe McDonald: 21,31
TOM STACK & ASSOCIATES / John Cancalosi: 22,24
Robert & Linda Mitchell: 28

Library of Congress Cataloging-in-Publication Data
Patton, Don
Iguanas / Don Patton.
p. cm.
Includes index.
ISBN 1-56766-190-4
1. Iguanas – Juvenile literature
[1. Iguanas.] I. Title.
QL666.L25P38 1995   95-7857
597.95 – dc20   CIP
                                                  AC